Wonders

Program Authors

Diane August	Jan Hasbrouck
Donald R. Bear	Margaret Kilgo
Janice A. Dole	Jay McTighe
Jana Echevarria	Scott G. Paris
Douglas Fisher	Timothy Shanahan
David Francis	Josefina V. Tinajero
Vicki Gibson	

McGraw Hill Education

Cover and Title pages: Nathan Love

www.mheonline.com/readingwonders

Copyright © 2017 McGraw-Hill Education

Send all inquiries to:
McGraw-Hill Education
2 Penn Plaza
New York, NY 10121

ISBN: 978-0-07-677828-7
MHID: 0-07-677828-2

Printed in the United States of America.

3 4 5 6 7 8 9 RMN 20 19 18 17 16

A

Unit 10 Thinking Outside the Box

The Big Idea: How can new ideas help us?

SOCIAL STUDIES

SCIENCE

SOCIAL STUDIES

(t) Jo Parry; (c) Holli Conger; (b) SW Productions/Photodisc/Getty Images

Essential Question
What can happen when
we work together?

Go Digital!

Teamwork!

Talk About It

How are these children working together?

Say the name of each picture.

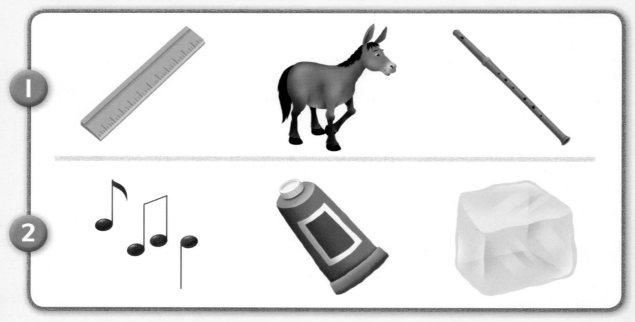

Read each word.

3 **use**   **rule**   **cute**

4 **rude**   **tube**   **cube**

Read Together

who	good

Who can use the paint?

You did a **good** job!

(t)KidStock/age fotostock; (b)©Andrea Ruester/Corbis

7

A Good Time for Luke!

Jo Parry

Luke is five.
He can run quick.
We like to play with Luke.

Jo Parry

Set up a date for Luke!

Jot Luke a quick note.

We can have a **good** time.

We are here for Luke.
Deb can set it up, up, up!
Tim has a bit of tape to fix
a rip.

Jo Parry

Mike can make a big cake.
He can make it in a tin pan.
June can use a red tube.

Look! June can tape it up on top.
Luke can take it home.
Luke is a fun kid in luck!

Jo Parry

Who can get Luke?
Where can we hide?
Luke will like it a lot!

Luke can see Deb, Tim,
Mike, June, and Kate.
Luke can have fun.
We have fun with Luke!

Jo Parry

15

Write About the Text

A Good Time for Luke!

Pages 8–15

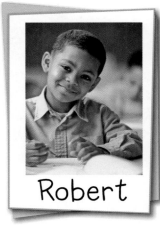

Robert

I responded to the prompt: **Write another story about children working together to celebrate a friend's birthday.**

Student Model: *Narrative Text*

It is Tom's birthday tomorrow. My friends Dan and Mel want to have a party for him. We all made a big card for Tom. The words that we wrote are very special.

Specific Words

I used the word **special** to describe the words we wrote.

Happy Birthday to a great friend

Andersen Ross/Blend Images/Getty Images

Events

I told how we got ready for the party as in the story.

Dan decorated a cake with soccer balls. Mel blew up balloons. We surprised Tom! He was really happy. We laughed and had a great time!

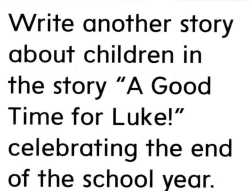

Grammar

The word **we** is a **pronoun**.

Your Turn

COLLABORATE

Write another story about children in the story "A Good Time for Luke!" celebrating the end of the school year.

Go Digital!
Write your response online.
Use your editing checklist.

Essential Question

In what ways are things alike? How are they different?

Go Digital!

Talk About It

Why is it helpful to sort things?

Richard Donovan/Alamy

A Place for Everything

Say the name of each picture.

Read each word.

3 me   see   be   Eve

4 seed   fee   beet   Pete

come   **does**

We will **come** to New York.

Does this bus go north?

We Come on Time!

We sit in a line.

It can take gas and time.

We do not need to be late.

Holli Conger

Jan and Pete can take
a bus.
Kim **does** not have to ride.
Kim does not see Pete.

Tom can ride a red bike.
He can go up, up, up.
But it is a quick ride to get
back home.

Dad has a job at a dock.
He can take Tim in a van.
Tim will not **come** late.

If it is wet, a van can help.
Dad can fit five in the van.
Dad can help a kid who
does not have a ride.

Holli Conger

If it is not wet, do not ride.
Lee and Kim can run,
run, run.
Pat can zip, zip quick, too!

We come in at the
same time.
We get in and sit on time.
Pat can get in line quick!

Write About the Text

Pages 22–29

Nina

I answered the question: **Why do the children come to school in different ways?**

Student Model: *Informative Text*

The children live in different places. Some children do not live near the school. They leave home early. They need to take a bus to school. Some children come with their parents by car.

Details
I used details to figure out that some children ride in a car.

Complete Sentences
My sentences tell complete ideas.

Other children live near the school. They can ride a bike to school. They can walk or run to school. These children can get home quickly!

Grammar

The word **they** is a **pronoun.**

Your Turn

How do the different ways you get to school help you make friends?

Go Digital!
Write your response online.
Use your editing checklist.

31

Essential Question

What ideas can you suggest to protect the environment?

Go Digital!

COLLABORATE

Talk About It

How are these children helping to protect our planet?

32

KidStock/age fotostock

Save the Planet!

Review Letter Sounds

Say the name of each picture.

Read each word.

3   **cake**   **bone**   **kite**   **Pete**

4   **rope**   **use**   **ate**   **meet**

Nathan Jarvis

Review Words

Read the words and sentences.

1 help   too   play   has

2 where   look   who

3 good   come   does

4 **Does** Mike want to **help**, **too**?

5 **Come** and **look** at my plant!

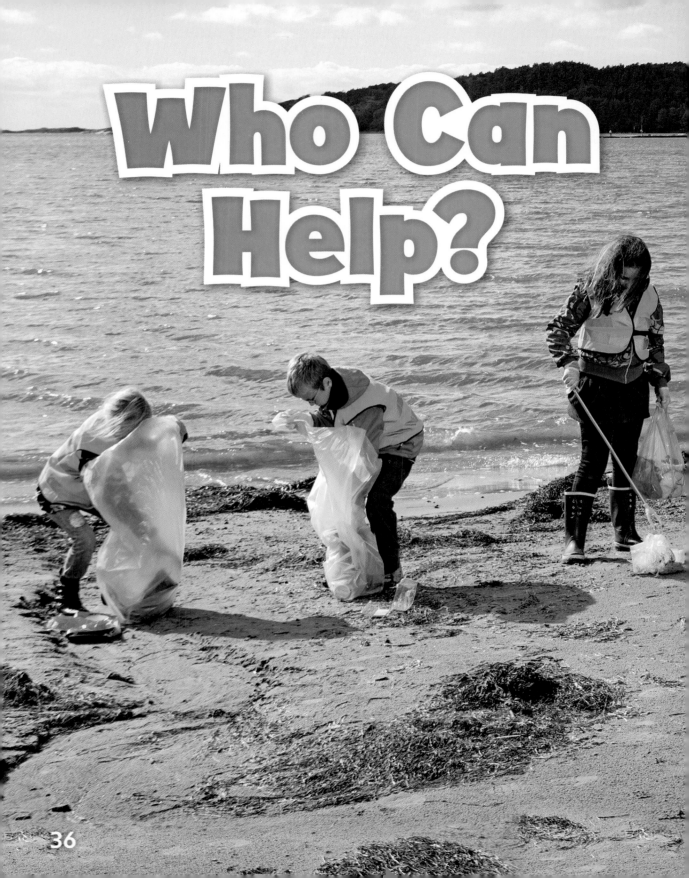

Who Can Help?

Dad **has** a big job.
He can do quite a lot.
Who can **help** Dad save
a lake?

Use a box, not a bag.
You can fit a lot in a box.
Yum, a kid can pack a
good box, **too** .

A mom can **come** and go.
It can take a lot of gas
to go.
But we save time and gas.

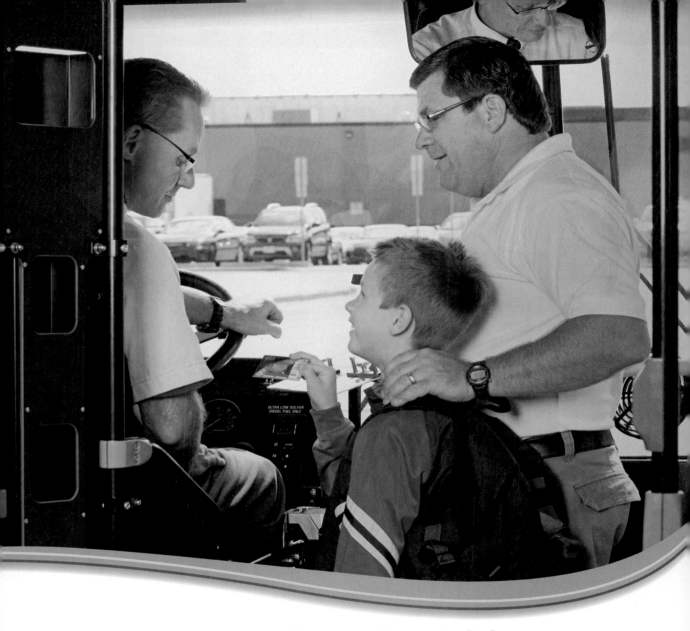

We can take a bus ride.
It can get us back home.
A bus can take a lot of us
where we like to go!

A kid can ride a bike.
It is fun to **play** like this.
It **does** not take gas to
ride, run, and hop.

A van can be a fun ride.
But it can use a lot of gas.
Look to see if five can fit
in the back!

See, a kid can do a lot!
A kid can fix. A kid
can save.
A little bit can help a lot.

43

Write About the Text

Pages 36–43

Dan

I responded to the prompt: **Write a letter to a friend telling how the helpers in "Who Can Help?" protect the environment.**

Student Model: *Informative Text*

Dear Martha,

I just read a great story called "Who Can Help?" It tells about how people help their environment. Children can use a lunch box instead of a bag. Anything used again can help the environment. Isn't that cool?

Grammar

The word **I** is a **pronoun.**

Facts

I included a detail from the selection.

Ken Cavanagh/McGraw-Hill Education

Topic
My sentences tell how the helpers protect their environment.

People can take a bus or a van to save gas. Both can take a lot of people. That's better than many people driving alone! The people are proud of how they help!

Best,

Dan

Your Turn

COLLABORATE

Look at the ideas in this selection. Then write a letter to a friend telling which ones you practice.

Go Digital!
Write your response online.
Use your editing checklist.

45